BUILT FOR SUCCESS

THE STORY OF

Target

Published by Creative Education
P.O. Box 227, Mankato, Minnesota 56002
Creative Education is an imprint of The Creative Company
www.thecreativecompany.us

DESIGN BY **ZENO DESIGN**
PRODUCTION BY **CHELSEY LUTHER**
ART DIRECTION BY **CHRISTINE VANDERBEEK**
Printed in the United States of America

PHOTOGRAPHS BY Alamy (Randy Duchaine, M4OS Photos,
Zoonar GmbH, ZUMA Press, Inc.), Corbis (Carlos Barria/Reuters,
MIKE BLAKE/Reuters, Naljah Feanny, Kenneth Johansson,
James Leynse), Getty Images (American Stock, Victor J. Blue/
Bloomberg, Lake County Museum, Craig Lassig/Bloomberg,
David Paul Morris/Bloomberg, Chip Somodevilla, Matthew
Staver/Bloomberg, Justin Sullivan, Mario Tama), Minnesota
Historical Society (Norton & Peel), Newscom (HENNY RAY
ABRAMS/AFP, Brendan Fitterer/ZUMApress)

LIBRARY OF CONGRESS CATALOGING-IN-PUBLICATION DATA
Gilbert, Sara.
The story of Target / Sara Gilbert.
p. cm. — (Built for success)
Summary: A look at the origins, leaders, growth, and products
of Target Corporation, the discount retailer founded in 1962,
which is the second-largest discount retailer in the United
States today.
Includes bibliographical references and index.
ISBN 978-1-60818-397-5
1. Target Corporation. 2. Department stores—United States—
Juvenile literature. 3. Stores, Retail—United States—Juvenile
literature. 4. Discount houses (Retail trade)—United States—
Juvenile literature. I. Title.

HF5465.U64T374 2014
381'.14106573—dc23   2013029652

CCSS: RI.5.1, 2, 3, 8; RH.6-8.4, 5, 6, 8

First Edition
9 8 7 6 5 4 3 2 1

THE STORY OF

Target

SARA GILBERT

On the morning of May 1, 1962, the first Target store opened in a renovated retail building on the corner of Snelling Avenue and Highway 36 in Roseville, Minnesota. Shoppers accustomed to perusing Target's pricier sister store, Dayton's, rushed through the doors to push red carts through the wide, clean aisles and peruse the discounted prices on everything from groceries and clothing to appliances and auto supplies. They even found innovative electronics in a department that included several selections of the latest rage: FM radios. As they filled their carts with goods, the checkout lines grew longer and longer. To help keep things moving, **executives** from The Dayton Company manned additional cash registers; corporate staffers even volunteered to bag the merchandise for customers.

CHAPTER ONE

Taking Aim

The Dayton family had been in the retail business since 1902, when George Draper Dayton and a partner opened Goodfellow's Dry Goods in a six-story building in downtown Minneapolis, Minnesota. With an orchestra serenading customers and well-dressed clerks happily ringing up their purchases of everything from fine clothing and jewelry to blankets, carpets, and curtains, the store soon became a popular venue.

Within a year, Dayton had bought out his partner and switched out Goodfellow's with his own name. In 1911, he renamed the store once again, now calling it The Dayton Company.

Dayton, his sons, and his grandsons spent the next several decades building that business on the corner of Nicollet Avenue and Seventh Street in Minneapolis. It doubled in size and turned a tidy **profit** every year. Eventually, it became clear that the store needed to expand its reach. In 1954, the company opened the first **branch** store in nearby Rochester, Minnesota, and in 1956, it built the first enclosed shopping mall in the country, with a Dayton's store anchoring one end of it, in the Minneapolis suburb of Edina.

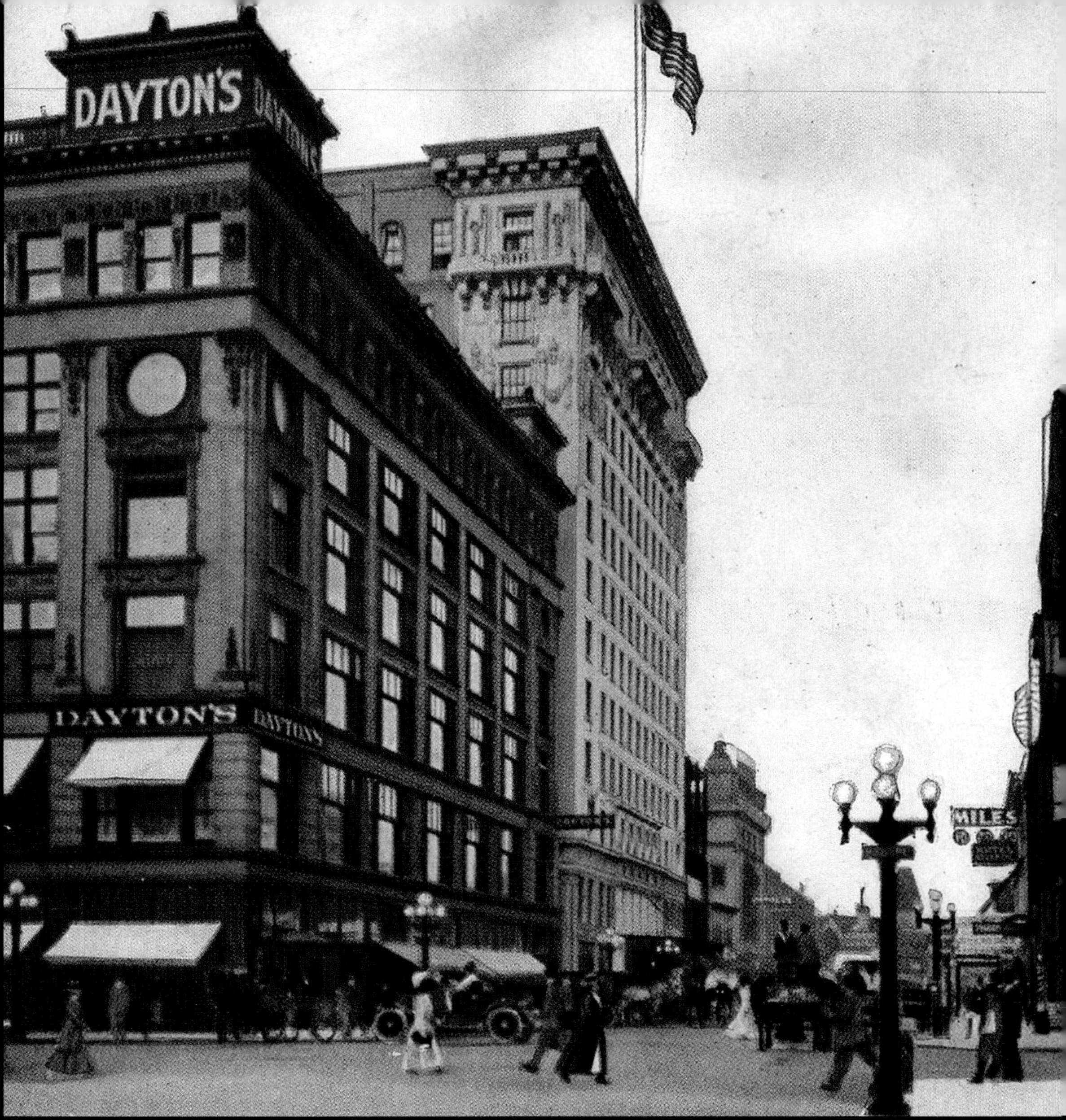
DAYTON'S
DAYTON'S
DAYTON'S
MILES

But Dayton's was known as an upscale retail outlet, and in the late 1950s and early 1960s, shopping trends seemed to be shifting toward discount retailing. In 1960, the Dayton family saw an opportunity to enlarge their business by transferring the successful Dayton's format to a discount store. The new stores, they decided in 1962, would be called Target, and they would maintain the reputation Dayton's had built for having a clean atmosphere, friendly service, and quality products. The biggest difference would be the discount prices. "Kmart was founded by a dime-store company, Wal-Mart was a variety store company," said longtime Target executive Norman McMillan. "The background of the Target enterprise was the department store business—so that influenced our strategic planning and the way the stores were run."

The Dayton Company invested $4 million, and Target president Douglas Dayton and his team dedicated hundreds of hours to preparing to launch the first four Target stores in 1962. Their goals were to stock the stores with new, interesting, high-quality products and to keep the prices for those products low by cutting expenses and reducing their profit **margins**.

The first store opened in the St. Paul suburb of Roseville in May; that was followed by stores in the Minneapolis suburbs of St. Louis Park and Crystal, then another in Duluth—a city with a population of approximately 106,000 located a little more than 3 hours north of Minneapolis–St. Paul.

Those four stores sold more than $11.4 million of merchandise in their first year of business—not quite enough to break even with expenses. In fact, the Target division suffered a loss of more than $600,000 its first year. And because the store's purchasing division had miscalculated how much of certain products to order, they found themselves with almost $1 million in extra **inventory** at year's end that had to be sold on clearance in 1963. But by 1964, they had figured out the ordering process and streamlined their systems. Sales soared to $27 million, bringing in a profit of $630,000 for the company.

Although the other new discount stores, including Kmart and Wal-Mart, were

Roseville, Minnesota, was home to the first Target store, which became a SuperTarget in 2005

TARGET

quickly expanding from city to city, the Daytons stayed closer to home for the first few years. They didn't open another store until 1965, when they added a location in the Minneapolis suburb of Bloomington. The next year, they opened their first out-of-state store in Denver, Colorado, because Dayton had heard that a competitor was planning to launch a new store using the Target logo in that city. Target moved in quickly, taking over space in a downtown storefront and stocking the shelves with $29 worth of products they had purchased at a nearby Walgreens.

Those Target stores were doing so well that at one point, Douglas Dayton walked into the office of his older brother Bruce, who had become the chief executive officer (CEO) of The Dayton Company in 1965, and predicted that Target would soon be a $100-million company. Both Bruce and Kenneth, another Dayton brother, laughed at what they thought was a ridiculous suggestion. They would be happy if the Target stores brought in $50 million.

But they agreed with Douglas that, to continue making money, they needed to expand Target's reach. After opening two more stores in Denver in 1966, they needed more money to invest in the division. In an effort to help raise those funds, on October 18, 1967, they sold 450,000 **shares** of the company, which became known as The Dayton Corporation, for $34 apiece on the **stock** market. That money helped finance two new Minnesota stores in 1967. It also allowed the company to begin looking into potential markets for expansion. In the summer of 1968, Target announced the grand opening of two new stores in St. Louis, Missouri.

By the end of 1968, Douglas Dayton was enjoying the last laugh. Sales for the 11 total Target stores had topped the improbable $100-million mark—prompting Dayton to up his prediction to $1 billion. "I am thoroughly convinced that we are producing a superior product which will bear the test of time," he told company executives that year.

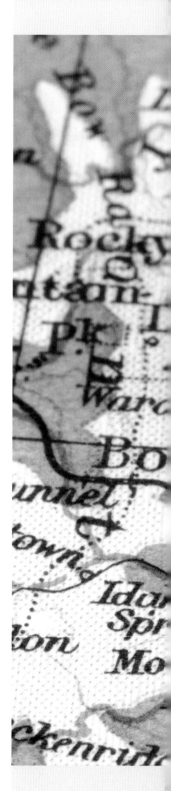

Minnesota-based Target decided to open its first out-of-state store in Denver, Colorado

Shoppers in the United States were introduced to several new stores in 1962—and they were all centered on the concept of offering a variety of products at the lowest prices possible. The first Kmart opened on March 1 in Garden City, Michigan. A month later, ShopKo was founded in Green Bay, Wisconsin. In May, Target's Roseville store opened its doors, and in June, the first Woolco store—covering more than 100,000 square feet with a parking lot that could hold 5,000 cars—opened in Columbus, Ohio. On July 2, a much smaller store was founded in the tiny town of Rogers, Arkansas. At that time, it was known as Wal-Mart Discount City—but today, it is well known around the world as Wal-Mart. Four of the five stores that debuted in 1962 are still in operation. Only Woolco no longer exists in the U.S.; it closed all its stores in 1982.

CHAPTER TWO

A Better Target

Douglas Dayton oversaw Target's expansion into Texas and Oklahoma in 1969, when the chain's total number of stores grew to 17. But in 1970, he was asked to serve as the senior vice president of administration for Dayton-Hudson Corporation, the new name of the parent company after its **merger** with Detroit-based department store J. L. Hudson in 1969.

It was too much of a desk job for Douglas, who had enjoyed being active in the day-to-day operations of Target, and he decided to leave the company.

Target continued an ambitious expansion plan under new president William Hodder. Between buying a line of existing stores that was going out of business and building its own stores, the chain grew to include 46 stores in 1972. But in the process, it began to experience its first growing pains. Profits were dropping, due in part to the costs associated with such rapid growth. Target was also struggling to meet the needs of customers in different parts of the country; snowsuits and shovels that sold well in Minnesota, for example, often ended up in southern states as well, where they weren't needed at all. And although product purchasing was all handled out of corporate headquarters in Minneapolis, many of the individual

ROSES

18.99

Expect More. Pay Less

Target continues to be mindful of how its storefront designs can complement the locale

stores were making independent decisions about the look and feel of their own locations.

Some stores had done their own decorating, hanging wooden shingles on the walls or hiring carpenters to create a new look for the store. Floors were often dirty, and merchandise was displayed in haphazard ways. Employees weren't being held to the high standards of customer service that the corporate office expected. And some of the inventory in the stores was becoming out of date and lingering on shelves too long. The high-quality, department-store feeling of the original Target stores was beginning to be lost.

To rein in those rogue stores, and to revitalize the Target brand, a new executive team was crafted that included Stephen Pistner, Kenneth Macke, and Norman McMillan. McMillan was charged with developing a written plan for the company that would define its identity, its goals, and its expectations of both the stores and their employees. That document, called *Guides for Growth*, was based on a series of principles that shaped every decision made by the chain—from a commitment to honesty and family values to customer service and the importance of employees. "In all my years in business, I don't recall a better document to guide a business by," Pistner said. "People who worked at Target knew who they were when they read that document."

As *Guides for Growth* was introduced to the **managers** of each store across the country, the company made a conscious decision to scale back its growth plan and focus on making the existing branches as profitable as possible. That meant that they had to cut prices even more deeply, just to get rid of inventory that wasn't selling well so that new products could be brought in instead. When new product was brought in, it was displayed in a uniform way, thanks to the "planograms" that had been introduced in 1974 to help ensure the same shopping experience at every store. The planograms, which laid out the exact placement of product throughout the store, made it easier for employees to keep the stores clean and uncluttered and simplified the stocking process.

Stocking the same products and shelving them in similar areas keeps Target stores unified

By 1975, the turnaround was complete: sales at Target stores grew to $511 million, making Target the number-one **revenue** producer for the Dayton-Hudson Corporation (at that point, Dayton-Hudson also owned B. Dalton Bookseller, Dayton Jewelers, and Dayton Development Company, in addition to Target and the Dayton's department stores). Now that it was back on track, Target could continue its expansion throughout the midsection of the United States. In 1976, four new Targets opened; seven were added in 1977, and another eight opened in 1978—including the first as part of a shopping mall, in Grand Forks, North Dakota. By the end of 1979, a total of 74 Target stores were operating in 11 states.

In 1979, the bold prediction Douglas Dayton had made just a decade earlier was realized: Target topped $1 billion in annual sales, ending the year with sales of $1.12 billion. But neither Douglas nor any of his brothers was around to celebrate the milestone this time. After successfully bringing in talented managers to lead each division of the corporation, the brothers relinquished their managerial responsibilities. Although Bruce and Kenneth Dayton remained on the **board of directors** for the Dayton-Hudson Corporation until 1983, their involvement in the everyday operations of the company was limited.

The Target stores, however, were eager to commemorate the achievement with a celebration. And this time, they included their customers. The "Billion Dollar Sale" that was held at all 74 of the stores in operation was a thank-you to everyone who had helped contribute to that success. "You and your friends bought a billion dollars' worth of bargains at Target in the past 12 months," the cover of the store's weekly flier announcing the sale proclaimed. "No matter how big we grow, we'll keep trying to be the best in town for value."

> *"When I'm traveling on tour, one of my favorite things to do is to throw a baseball cap on and go to a Target."*
>
> SINGER CHRISTINA AGUILERA

B. Dalton bookstores, founded by Dayton's and sold to Barnes & Noble, were closed in 2013

HITTING A BULL'S-EYE

When Stewart K. Widdess, the director of publicity for Dayton's, was asked to come up with a name and identity for the company's new discount store in 1962, he gathered his staff together and asked for suggestions. More than 200 possible names were thrown out before "Target" was mentioned. Almost as soon as the idea had been floated, Widdess's team envisioned using a classic red-and-white bull's-eye as the logo. But it took several drafts to come up with the right version. "We even had one target with three bullet holes through it—which even in the 1960s we decided wasn't appropriate," remembered Douglas Dayton, Target's first president. The logo he eventually approved depicted a target composed of three red rings. In 1968, that logo was updated to include just two red circles—one in the center and another around it. That logo, and the basic concept behind Target's identity, has remained unchanged ever since.

CHAPTER THREE

Covering the Country

As the 1980s began, Target and the Dayton-Hudson Corporation were considered among the top retailers in the U.S. The corporation as a whole turned a profit every year; Target, which had grown to 151 stores and sales of $2.05 billion by the end of 1981, was by far the most profitable of all its divisions. But at that point, Target was still considered a primarily midwestern company, because the majority of its locations were in Minnesota, Wisconsin, Iowa, Oklahoma, Missouri, North Dakota, and Indiana.

Early in the decade, Target set its sights on growing beyond the central section of the country. It took its first steps toward achieving that goal in 1982, with the **acquisition** of 33 existing FedMart department stores in Arizona, California, and Texas. FedMart owner Sol Price had built up a chain of 45 successful stores in the southwestern U.S., but in 1975 he sold them to a German retail chain that wasn't interested in maintaining the stores. That provided Target with an opportunity to establish an immediate presence in the West by renovating those stores and re-opening them with the red bull's-eye logo in 1983.

CAN I HELP YOU FIND SOMETHING?

More than 360,000 employees worldwide sport Target's signature red shirts

That westward expansion necessitated the building of a distribution center—a large warehouse where products were stored and then shipped to all the locations in that region—in Los Angeles. Target had built its first distribution center in 1969 in Fridley, Minnesota, near its cluster of stores in the "Twin Cities" metropolitan area of Minneapolis and St. Paul. It had since added two others (in Indianapolis, Indiana, and Little Rock, Arkansas). Incorporating the Los Angeles location helped spur further growth on the West Coast. In 1986, Target bought up another 30 existing department stores in California, making it the dominant retailer in Southern California. In 1988, it moved farther up the Pacific Coast, building eight stores in Washington and three in Oregon.

By the end of 1988, Target had 341 stores in 27 states. Its sales had soared to more than $5 billion a year, and Kenneth Macke, the chairman and CEO of Dayton-Hudson, had predicted that the chain would grow to include more than 400 stores by the end of 1989. But back at corporate headquarters in Minneapolis, total sales were flat, and some of the company's other divisions—including the line of Mervyn's department stores it had purchased in 1978—were struggling. The price of Dayton-Hudson Corporation's stock dropped.

That left the company vulnerable to an attempted **takeover** by an aggressive Maryland-based retail operation that had started secretly buying up large amounts of the company's stock in the spring of 1987. When that company—the Dart Group—and its investors proposed a merger of the two companies later that year, Dayton-Hudson rejected the offer, saying it was "inadequate and not in the best interests of the corporation and its shareholders, nor in the interests of its employees, customers, communities, and other constituencies." But the group of investors pursuing the takeover, who now owned a third of the company's stock, upped the bid.

Fearful that a hostile takeover was imminent, the leaders of Dayton-Hudson made a late-night call to the governor of Minnesota, Rudy Perpich, to make an odd request: They wanted him to convene a special session of the state

By the 1980s, Target stores were becoming familiar sights in locations across the U.S.

legislature and introduce a **bill** that would toughen the state's laws regarding hostile takeovers. At the time, Dayton-Hudson was Minnesota's largest company; it employed 34,000 people in the state. The governor recognized that losing ownership of the company could have a negative effect on the state's **economy**, and six days later, he called the lawmakers together to vote on the proposed law. Many of those legislators had shopped at Target or Dayton's; many also knew that the company was extremely generous with the money it donated to arts organizations and other charities in the state. They passed the bill, and the governor signed it into law. "It's because of 84 years of good service, 84 years as an employer and corporate citizen of this state," state senator Roger Moe said after the law's passage. "We'd do it for anybody who has that same kind of reputation in this state."

Before that new law could be tested, however, the stock market crashed in October 1987, and the value of Dayton-Hudson's stock—as well as most others—plunged. The shares that the Dart Group had purchased were now worth less than half of what they had originally paid for them. As Dayton-Hudson jumped on the opportunity to buy those shares back at a greatly reduced price, the Dart Group withdrew its purchase offer.

With the takeover crisis over, Target could comfortably complete its bid to build stores from coast to coast. In 1989, the company shifted its focus to the southeastern U.S., adding stores in Kentucky, Tennessee, Florida, Georgia, North Carolina, and South Carolina. On one day in April, 30 new stores opened in the Southeast. The company trumpeted that saturation with a television advertising campaign that featured the country-music group The Judds, which was especially popular in that region. All told, 60 total sites were opened in the Southeast in 1989, bringing Target's total number of stores to 399.

"There's this whole 'Tarzhay' cult—they love the brand and consider it to be their little secret."

BILL OBERLANDER, AD EXECUTIVE

Born in 1944, Roger Moe served as a Minnesota state senator for more than 30 years

TARGET'S MARKETING MUSCLE

Target has been advertising its specials with a newspaper insert every week since 1962. That insert evolved from a two-color flier illustrated with line drawings into a full-color, glossy publication that reaches more than 50 million households each week. But the flier is just part of the company's marketing plan, which also includes television commercials, magazine and newspaper advertisements, and sponsorships of both events and buildings (including Target Field, home of the Minnesota Twins baseball team, and Target Center, home of the Minnesota Timberwolves basketball team). Most of its marketing revolves around the ubiquitous bull's-eye, which is so closely identified with Target that the store's name isn't even necessary to mention. When Target opened its first stores in New York City, it ran ads with just the logo and a line stating, "If you know what this symbol means ... call 888-100-1235." So many people called the number that it had to be taken down.

CHAPTER FOUR

From Great to Super

With almost 400 stores in 30 states across the country, Target started the 1990s focused on a different kind of expansion. Even as it continued opening new stores, it also began looking for opportunities to build on what had become one of the most respected brands in retailing.

On September 30, 1990, it introduced the first of its new concepts with the opening of a 169,000-square-foot (15,700 sq m) Target Greatland store in Apple Valley, Minnesota, a suburb of Minneapolis. Although it resembled typical Target stores in many ways, it was 50 percent larger and built to be even more of a shopping experience for customers. The aisles were wider, the clothing departments were located front and center, and convenient price scanners were scattered throughout the store. Although as much as 90 percent of the merchandise was the same, it was displayed in different ways; the menswear department, for example, featured tables of folded clothing and shelves reaching almost seven feet up the wall.

The Target Greatland concept was conceived especially to give the store a leg up in highly competitive markets (such as Chicago) where it hadn't yet experienced success. It opened 43 more Greatland units in 1991 and had plans to build 50 more of the stores in the Chicago area within the next 5 years.

Shopping carts at Greatland and other Targets got a makeover from the old models (shown) in 2006.

Some of the other new ideas that Target tried, however, weren't as well-received. In 1992, it opened a pair of specialty clothing stores called Everyday Hero in the Minneapolis area, hoping to compete with such established clothing retailers as GAP. Five years later, both stores—including one in the Mall of America, the company's only presence there—closed. In 1993, it launched Smarts, a chain of closeout stores designed to help reduce clearance inventory that was building up in its distribution centers. Just two years after opening the four Smarts locations—one each in California, Texas, Iowa, and Indiana—Target abandoned the concept and closed them all.

As it shuttered those stores in 1995, it made its move into the "supercenter" field with the introduction of SuperTarget, which added a grocery section for fresh produce, dairy products, meat, and non-perishable goods to the traditional Target format. Target's main competitors—Wal-Mart and Kmart—had already established themselves as the supercenter leaders: Wal-Mart had 150 open at the time, with plans to add 100 more within the year, and Kmart had more than 70. Target would have to play catch-up to remain competitive with those chains, but it took a cautious approach to the concept. "We think it's a strategy worth testing," a Target spokeswoman said at the time. "We see that when people have less time, one-stop shopping becomes a convenience. It seems like a strategy that can work."

The first SuperTarget, a 190,000-square-foot (17,652 sq m) store with 65 checkout lanes, opened in Omaha, Nebraska, in March 1995. The second was built in Lawrence, Kansas, later that year. Four more opened the following year. Although it was a successful venture, Target maintained its slow approach to building more stores. Within a decade, it had just more than 200 SuperTarget locations in 22 states; Wal-Mart had 239 by the end of 1995.

Throughout all its new ventures, Target remained committed to expanding the reach of its traditional discount stores as well. It had become one of the top three discount retailers in the country and was committed to maintaining that

To meet growing customer demands for one-stop shopping, SuperTargets contained grocery sections

reputation. By 1995, it had a total of 670 stores; a year later, it had 736. By the end of 1997, almost 800 Target stores brought in sales of more than $20 billion.

Of that total, Target donated 5 percent—approximately $1 billion—to schools and charities in the communities in which it did business. The store had made a commitment to give back when it started and had also established the Good Neighbor program, which provided opportunities for its employees to volunteer. In 1997, U.S. president Bill Clinton awarded Target the President's Service Award, the highest national honor for corporate volunteer efforts.

Despite that national recognition, there was still one section of the country that still hadn't heard of Target: the northeast, and particularly the New York City metropolitan area. Once again, Target found itself behind its competition, as both Wal-Mart and Kmart had sites in Manhattan by then. Instead of joining them in New York's busiest **borough**, Target decided to open its first New York City store in Queens—a more residential borough than Manhattan—in 1998. "We're kind of oriented to where people drive up in a car and load it up with a cart full of stuff," the company's CEO Bob Ulrich said.

That same year, Target opened locations in Pennsylvania, New Jersey, and elsewhere in New York. In 1999, it landed in the Boston metropolitan area, bringing its total number of stores to 912 in 44 states. It also had one store with no geographic location at all: On September 7, 1999, it launched a virtual store on the World Wide Web. And by the end of the year, it had achieved sales of $26 billion—representing three-quarters of the total revenue brought in by the Dayton-Hudson Corporation.

"*The Dayton brothers did everything morally, ethically, and culturally exactly the way it should have been done.*"

ALLAN PENNINGTON, FORMER TARGET VICE PRESIDENT

Target's website, which launched in 1999, gave customers a new way to browse—and buy

George Draper Dayton's great-grandson Mark became governor in 2011

THE DAYTON BROTHERS

In 1950, George Draper Dayton's six grandsons took over the business that he had started in 1902. Those five brothers—Bruce, Douglas, Donald, Kenneth, and Wallace—and cousin George II agreed that the company needed to grow beyond its department store in downtown Minneapolis. "One store wasn't big enough for five boys," Bruce Dayton said. "We had to figure out a growth plan." They started by adding new branches of the Dayton's department store, including one in the nearby cities of St. Paul, Rochester, and Edina. They also launched the successful Target chain of stores, and had the foresight to surround themselves with talented executives who would lead the business in their absence. By 1978, each of the brothers had moved on to different ventures, turning the management of the business over to others. "I would describe them as bright, hardworking, driven, and really, they drove each other," said former Target executive Norman McMillan.

CHAPTER FIVE

Target Takes Over

When the opening bell sounded on the New York Stock Exchange on the morning of January 31, 2000, shares of the Dayton-Hudson Corporation were being traded under a new name: Target Corporation. The company had decided that the new name better reflected the direction in which the business was headed. More than 70 percent of its total stores were Targets, and more than 75 percent of its revenue came from those stores.

And Target, with its bold logo, had become far more recognizable than any of the other divisions. Even Bruce Dayton, whose family had been the namesake of the business since 1902, thought it was a good decision. "I think it's a very positive move," he said.

The name changes didn't end there. Barely a year later, Target Corporation announced that the Dayton's and Hudson's department stores would all take the name Marshall Field's, a venerable line of stores founded in Chicago which the company had purchased in 1990, because that name was better known throughout the rest

Target Corporation shareholders can check daily stock market reports on the company's worth

of the country. Now there were just three divisions in the company: Target, which had 1,053 stores by the end of 2001; Marshall Field's, with 62 stores; and Mervyn's, which had 266 stores.

Although Target was expanding—it had moved into Maine, its 47th state, in 2001—and bringing in more than $40 billion in sales in 2003, the other two divisions were struggling. In the spring of 2004, the company decided that the best course of action would be to sell both divisions. By June, Marshall Field's was sold to May Department Stores, which operated the Macy's line of stores. A month later, an investment group bought all the Mervyn's stores as well.

Many were disappointed to see the company abandon the department store format that had been its roots, while others saw the change as an opportunity for Target to more directly challenge its competition—especially Wal-Mart. With no other distractions, Target took an aggressive approach to expansion in 2004 and 2005, opening more than 170 stores in that span. By the end of 2005, the company had reached another major milestone, earning more than $50 billion a year for the first time.

But as Target was ramping up its growth efforts—opening an average of one new store every four days—the economy in the U.S. was taking a downward plunge. When a **recession** happened in 2008, Target was one of many corporations that was hit hard. In November, sales were down by almost 10 percent over the previous year, and the values of the company's stock had dropped by more than 60 percent. Shoppers had certainly become more **frugal** and weren't buying as much, but Target was also running into trouble with the credit cards it had been issuing to customers who were now unable to pay their bills.

Target responded by changing the content of its weekly advertisements to promote exceptionally low prices on everyday products rather than on just the more discretionary—or non-necessary—items it often featured. By the end of 2008, Target was spending three-quarters of its marketing budget in promoting value-priced items. It also started paying attention to what its competitors

On Thanksgiving Day 2012, Target opened at 9 P.M., the earliest ever, for Black Friday shoppers

were charging for the same products. When Wal-Mart, which had a reputation for offering lower prices than Target, slashed prices on toys in 2009, for example, Target did the same. Those efforts helped: In December 2009, Target's same-store sales (a comparison among stores that have been open at least a year) had grown by a modest 1.8 percent. Holiday sales that year were up nearly 5 percent over the previous year.

Despite the economic downturn, Target went ahead with the grand openings of new stores in Alaska and Hawaii—the 48th and 49th states to become home to Target. The only state without a Target store as of 2013 was Vermont, a small state that had historically taken a stand against giving big-box retailers space in its quaint small towns. Although Wal-Mart had succeeded in establishing a location there, Target had not had any luck in receiving permission from the state government to build a store.

Instead of dwelling on that, Target decided to expand into Canada instead. To make its move north of the border, the company purchased the leases on more than 200 stores owned by the Canadian chain Zellers in 2011. The majority of those remodeled spaces opened as Targets in the spring of 2013. Other international expansion, including into sites in Asia and Europe, was also being discussed.

Target continued to look for new ways to reach its customers in the U.S. as well. In 2012, it started opening CityTarget locations—smaller stores in downtown areas with a more **urban** feel than the more than 1,760 sprawling, suburban stores for which the chain was best known. CityTargets opened in Los Angeles, Chicago, San Francisco, and Seattle in 2012, with more slated to open in the coming years.

For more than 50 years, Target has remained committed to its founders' vision of offering high-quality merchandise at bargain prices—and shoppers have rewarded that commitment with almost unwavering loyalty to the store. With a long history of retail success to support it, Target will continue to keep those customers coming back for decades to come.

> "I love to go shopping at Target. They have so much stuff there, you can buy almost anything. It's really amazing."
>
> ACTRESS LIV TYLER

city ◎
10861

Target hoped the smaller-sized, urban CityTarget stores would expand its customer demographics

TARGET AUDIENCE

The Dayton brothers envisioned Target as more upscale and quality-based than the other discount stores that were established at the same time—a vision that helped shape the clientele who shop there. Target shoppers tend to be younger, more educated, and wealthier than the shoppers at such competitors as Wal-Mart. According to Target's website in 2013, the average Target "guest" was 40 years old and female; less than a quarter of the store's customers were male. Not quite half (43 percent) of Target's guests have children. Almost 80 percent of Target shoppers have attended some college, and more than half of them (57 percent) received a college degree. The median household income was approximately $64,000. But perhaps the most important statistic for a retail chain with almost 1,800 stores in 49 states may be that approximately 97 percent of the consumers in the U.S. recognize its bright red bull's-eye logo.

GLOSSARY

acquisition the purchase of one company by another

bill the written draft of a proposed law presented to a governmental body for discussion

board of directors a group of people in charge of making decisions for a publicly owned company

borough one of the five divisions of New York City

branch a distinct location of the same business venture

economy the system of producing, distributing, and consuming goods within a society

executives decision-making leaders of a company, such as the president or chief executive officer (CEO)

frugal careful with money, especially regarding spending it

inventory the total of a company's merchandise that has not yet been sold

managers the people responsible for controlling all or part of a company's operations

margins amounts of profit expected on certain products

marketing the process of promoting products or services

merger the combination of two companies into one

profit the amount of money that a business keeps after subtracting expenses from income

recession a period of decline in the financial stability of a country or society that typically includes a drop in the stock market, an increase in unemployment, and a decline in home sales

revenue the money earned by a company; another word for income

shares the equal parts a company may be divided into; shareholders each hold a certain number of shares, or a percentage, of the company

sponsorships agreements to pay some or all of the costs involved in an event or building project in exchange for advertising

stock shared ownership in a company by many people who buy shares, or portions, of stock, hoping the company will make a profit and the stock value will increase

takeover the act of taking control of something, as in when one company buys out another company

urban relating to the characteristics of a city

SELECTED BIBLIOGRAPHY

Carpenter, Donna Sammons. *Right on Target*. Upper Saddle River, N.J.: New Word City, 2010.

Levinson, Marc. "The Year that Changed Retailing Forever." *Bloomberg News*, May 15, 2012. http://www.bloomberg.com /news/2012-05-15/the-year-that-changed-retailing-forever .html.

Malcolm, Hadley, and Jane O'Donnell. "Discount Birthday: Wal-Mart, Kmart, Target Hit 50." *USA Today*, September 17, 2012.

Rowley, Laura. *On Target: How the World's Hottest Retailer Hit a Bull's-Eye*. Hoboken, N.J.: John Wiley & Sons, 2003.

Target Corporation. "Corporate Fact Sheet." http://pressroom .target.com/corporate.

Target Corporation. "Target through the Years." https:// corporate.target.com/about/history/.

Note: Every effort has been made to ensure that any websites listed above were active at the time of publication. However, because of the nature of the Internet, it is impossible to guarantee that these sites will remain active indefinitely or that their contents will not be altered.

INDEX